Global Network: Computers in a Sustainable Society

JOHN E. YOUNG

Aaron Sachs, *Staff Researcher*

Ed Ayres, *Editor*

WORLDWATCH PAPER 115
September 1993

THE WORLDWATCH INSTITUTE is an independent, nonprofit environmental research organization based in Washington, D.C. Its mission is to foster a sustainable society—in which human needs are met in ways that do not threaten the health of the natural environment or future generations. To this end, the Institute conducts interdisciplinary research on emerging global issues, the results of which are published and disseminated to decisionmakers and the media.

FINANCIAL SUPPORT is provided by the Geraldine R. Dodge Foundation, George Gund Foundation, W. Alton Jones Foundation, John D. and Catherine T. MacArthur Foundation, Andrew W. Mellon Foundation, Curtis and Edith Munson Foundation, Edward John Noble Foundation, Pew Charitable Trusts, Lynn R. and Karl E. Prickett Fund, Public Welfare Foundation, Rockefeller Brothers Fund, Surdna Foundation, Turner Foundation, and Frank Weeden Foundation.

PUBLICATIONS of the Institute include the annual *State of the World*, which is now published in 27 languages; *Vital Signs*, an annual compendium of the global trends—environmental, economic, and social—that are shaping our future; the *Environmental Alert* book series; and *World Watch* magazine, as well as the *Worldwatch Papers*. For more information on Worldwatch publications, write: Worldwatch Institute, 1776 Massachusetts Ave., N.W., Washington, DC 20036; or FAX (202) 296-7635.

THE WORLDWATCH PAPERS provide in-depth, quantitative and qualitative analysis of the major issues affecting prospects for a sustainable society. The Papers are authored by members of the Worldwatch Institute research staff and reviewed by experts in the field. Published in five languages, they have been used as a concise and authoritative reference by governments, nongovernmental organizations and educational institutions worldwide. For a partial list of available Papers, see page 75.

Table of Contents

Tables and Figures

ACKNOWLEDGEMENTS: The author would like to thank Mark Bennett, Leslie Byster, Amanda Hawes, Paul Hyland, Gregory Pitts, Howard Rheingold, Ted Smith, and Michael Stein for reviewing preliminary drafts of this paper. Project oversight was provided by Christopher Flavin, vice president for research at Worldwatch.

JOHN E. YOUNG, a Senior Researcher at the Worldwatch Institute, studies pollution, waste, technology, and industrial policy issues. He is the author of Worldwatch Paper 109, *Mining the Earth*, and Paper 101, *Discarding the Throwaway Society*, and has also been a co-author of four of the Institute's annual *State of the World* reports. He is a graduate of Carleton College, where he studied political science and technology policy.

Introduction

Computers were born and raised by the armed forces, and popularized by the consumer economy. But their greatest value may prove to be neither military nor commercial. With the Cold War receding, it is now apparent that we are confronted by two even more overwhelming challenges: a faltering world economy that despite its huge reach and productivity we only poorly understand, and a deteriorating global environment whose vast workings we understand even less. Coming to grips with the great task of the twenty-first century—to reconcile hopes for global prosperity with the need for a healthy environment—will require a far more detailed understanding of both. Given how rapidly ecosystems are now declining, that understanding will have to be pursued far faster than it has been. It is in this pursuit that the computer may find its greatest application.

Computers were first applied to massive mathematical problems for which the military wanted answers, such as explaining the turbulence created by atomic explosions, or predicting the flight of artillery shells. They were later put to work on exhaustive civilian tasks involving the management of unwieldy amounts of information, such as computing the payrolls of large companies, or tabulating responses to census questionnaires. For a quarter-century, computers were regarded as exotic machines that could be operated—or understood—only by geniuses.[1]

But these machines have changed, and so have their roles. No longer the exclusive province of a technical priesthood, they are just beginning to fulfill their destined purpose as information organizers in an age of information glut. Their value lies in their ability to help us organize the overwhelming mass of raw industrial, economic, demographic, and scientific data society now generates into forms that can be used to solve problems—in other words, to turn *information* into *knowledge*. And nowhere is the need for knowledge greater than in the drive to create a sustainable global economy.

For all our expertise in building factories and transforming humble raw materials into technological marvels—and for all the uncounted volumes of statistics collected to track our efforts—we know remarkably little about how to produce what we need in a way that can be sustained. Though satellites now beam down thousands of volumes of data about the planet each day, the information remains largely unexamined—and bewildering. We are stuffed with information but starved for knowledge. Computers can provide an urgently needed service by sorting through the interconnected workings of extraordinarily complex systems, from factories to forests, to identify what is going wrong and develop corrective strategies. And they provide us with the means to test theories about those systems without conducting dangerous, often unintentional, global experiments, such as those now underway involving the addition of large amounts of pollutants to the atmosphere and biosphere.

The capacity of the computer to help us bridge the critical gap between information and knowledge is illustrated by the recent history of climate science. Scientists have theorized since 1896 that emissions of carbon dioxide from the burning of fossil fuels could warm the global atmosphere. Their concerns grew in the fifties, sixties and seventies, as increasing atmospheric concentrations of carbon dioxide and other gases were documented. It was not until the early 1980s, however—when computers sufficiently powerful for modeling the complex behavior of the atmosphere became available—that they were able to test their theories. Supercomputers at such centers as the Geophysical Fluid Dynamics Laboratory in Princeton, New Jersey, and the Goddard Institute of Space Studies in New York, have been programmed to simulate the effects of increased greenhouse gas concentrations on the global climate. In minutes, they perform calculations that would take an unaided scientist a lifetime or more.[2]

This computer-based modeling of the atmosphere has produced a remarkable consensus among climatologists about the
likelihood and potential scope of global warming. If—as those
scientists now predict—the earth's atmosphere warms by several degrees within the span of a few decades, there will be enormous impacts on the environment and the global economy.
Among the predicted impacts are a rise in sea levels that would
threaten coastal populations, and shifts in temperature and
rainfall patterns that could devastate agricultural areas and force
the migration or extinction of many of the earth's species.
Climatologists are also using computers to try to determine
from local temperature measurements whether such warming is
already beginning to occur. The task would be difficult or impossible without computers, since it involves a complex calculation
based on thousands of daily readings from around the world that
must be adjusted for a variety of complicating factors, including
the uneven geographical distribution of monitoring stations
and the tendency for urban areas—with their relative lack of trees
and abundance of pavement—to yield higher readings.[3]

Predicting or identifying an environmental problem is only
the first step in dealing with it. The governments of the world
have already agreed that global warming poses a major threat—
but they have only just begun to develop a response. Computers
can be used not only to identify the need for such a response,
but to shape it. For example, a computer model developed for
the U.S. Agency for International Development has been used by
government planners in Madagascar and the Philippines to
quickly predict and graphically present the economic and
resource consequences—including levels of carbon dioxide emissions—of various population growth scenarios. Other models
have helped environmentalists sketch out realistic plans for
reducing carbon dioxide emissions through more efficient energy use and the use of alternatives to fossil fuels, such as wind and
solar power. Computers already play an important role in making those new technologies possible. For example, high-effi-
ciency fluorescent lights—including most of the compact fluorescent bulbs now rapidly replacing traditional incandescents in
many buildings—contain computer chips that control their

function, as do the newest, most efficient wind and solar power equipment.[4]

Computer-based communications can also help broaden public participation in the debate on global warming and other environmental issues by making previously inaccessible environmental and industrial information widely available. Global computer networks have sharply accelerated communications among scientists—who can now collaborate on projects while working thousands of miles apart—and are now beginning to spread rapidly outside academic institutions. In the United States, publicly accessible databases on industrial pollution and alternative industrial technologies have become powerful tools for environmental and community groups. Even in some developing countries, computer networks are beginning to bring greater access to information—and political power—to impoverished or rural populations that in the past have been largely left out of the decisionmaking process. Such broad political participation will be crucial in the process of forging a more sustainable society. Without it, nations are unlikely to find the political will to dramatically cut energy and materials use, reduce industrial pollution, and preserve vital ecosystems.

The measure of any new technology extends beyond the benefits of applying it, however. The environmental and human costs of producing and using it must also be considered—and the costs of computerizing the globe are substantial. Swept up in our visions of the potential power of computers, we have failed to come to grips with their impacts.

Simply turning on a computer contributes to environmental problems, since electric power plants are major contributors to a variety of environmental problems, including global warming, acid rain, and destruction of natural habitats. Computers have become a major electricity consumer in industrial countries. And while it may be good for democracy that virtually anyone with a computer and a good printer can now become a publisher, the world's forests are none the better for it. Instead of creating the "paperless office" so optimistically predicted a decade ago, computers have stimulated an ever-growing demand for paper. Computer designers, programmers, and users have only just begun to address such problems.

Computer manufacturing, which has quickly grown into one of the world's largest, most powerful industries, also has environmental impacts that, until recently, have largely gone unrecognized. Few Americans realize, for example, that the "clean" or "sunrise" industry that arose in Silicon Valley has also created in its California birthplace the highest concentration of hazardous-waste cleanup sites in the United States. Electronics makers currently use a host of toxic substances, and have far to go in developing cleaner production processes that avoid both environmental damage and toxic risks to workers.

A New Technology, a New Industry

One reason the impacts of computers and their production have been little considered is that both the technology and the industry have evolved at an astonishing rate. The first electronic digital computer—the ENIAC of 1945—was made from more than 17,000 vacuum tubes in a cabinet 3 meters high, 2 meters deep, and 30 meters long. It weighed 27 tons. By today's standards, it was laughably low-powered. Since then, a series of basic technical advances has dramatically increased the computing power that can be packed into a given space. In the 1950s, transistors—which were much smaller—replaced vacuum tubes as the basic components of computers. In the 1960s, the development

The amount of computing power that can be purchased for a given price has been doubling every two years for three decades.

of integrated circuits allowed large numbers of transistors to be packed onto standardized circuit boards. Then, in 1971, came the microprocessor, a single thumbnail-sized chip of silicon onto which were etched thousands of microscopic transistors— enough for all the basic components of a computer.[5]

Microchips have allowed computers to evolve from room-sized to notebook- or even palm-sized devices. For instance, there are over *3 million* transistors on the Intel Corporation's newest microprocessor, the Pentium, upon which the fastest personal computers (PCs) are now based. If that thumbnail-sized piece of equipment were built of vacuum tubes, arranged like those in the original ENIAC computer, they would fill a three-mile-long line of the old 3-by-10-foot cabinets. Measured in MIPS (million instructions per second), a standard measure of a computer's ability to perform certain basic operations, machines based on the Pentium operate about 3,000 times as fast at certain basic calculations as an original 1981 International Business Machines (IBM) PC.[6]

Since the early 1980s, when personal computers began to catch on, rapidly increasing capabilities and plummeting prices have caused an explosive increase in the number of machines in use. The amount of computing power that can be purchased for a given price has been doubling every two years or less for three decades, making the computer easily available to many individuals and most institutions. There were probably fewer than 2 million computers in the world in 1980, most of them mainframes or somewhat smaller multi-user minicomputers. There are now an estimated 148 million, of which 135 million are PCs. Eighteen million of these were added in 1992 alone. And because new machines are orders of magnitude more powerful than the old, growth in global processing power is even more rapid. Measured in MIPS, the total power of the world's computers has risen elevenfold in the last six years.[7] (See Figure 1.)

The use of computers is heavily concentrated in the industrialized nations. There are 265 computers per 1000 people in the United States, 57 per 1000 in Italy, and only 1 per 1000 in China and India. The United States—where both the microprocessor and the personal computer were invented—has almost half the world's computers, though only a twentieth of the world's people. Computers may soon be more numerous there than cars, which have been perhaps the country's most dominant cultural artifact to date.[8] (See Table 1.)

A computer is useless without its programming, or software. The greatest profits in the computer industry are now made by software producers and by makers of the most sophisticated microprocessors, whose value lies largely in the basic programs

FIGURE 1.
World Computers and Total Processing Power, 1987–93

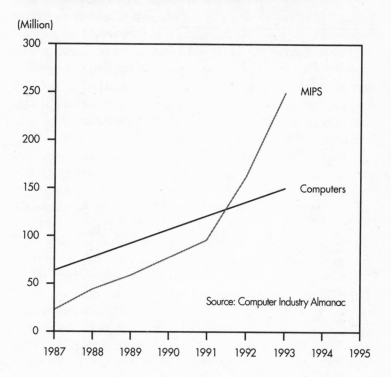

(Million)

Source: Computer Industry Almanac

etched within them. Today, the industry's most powerful firms are Microsoft Corporation, which sells only software, and Intel Corporation, which primarily sells microprocessors, including most of those that are the core of IBM-compatible PCs. And though Intel's and Microsoft's sales are still far lower than those of IBM—the dominant producer of entire machines—they now rival it in market value. Microsoft sells the most widely used operating system—the basic software which underpins all programs—for IBM-compatible computers. It now sells $2.8 billion worth of software each year, and its stock is valued at $22 billion. For the software industry as a whole, sales now exceed $45 billion per year. While billions of dollars worth of software for mainframes and centralized business computer systems are still

Table 1.
Computers and Computing Power, Various Countries, 1993

Country	Computers	MIPS[1]
	(per 1000 people)	
United States	265	516
Australia	175	278
Canada	162	264
Norway	153	256
Denmark	145	240
New Zealand	138	230
United Kingdom	134	217
Switzerland	133	220
Sweden	132	218
Ireland	126	208
Finland	122	202
Singapore	116	178
France	111	180
Belgium	110	183
Germany	104	141
Netherlands	97	161
Austria	85	140
Japan	84	139
Israel	81	133
Taiwan	68	110
Italy	57	98
Spain	50	76
Greece	47	71
Portugal	39	61
South Korea	33	49
Hungary	24	34
Saudi Arabia	22	34
Czechoslovakia	19	27
Mexico	13	19
Poland	12	19
South Africa	9	13
Brazil	6	10
USSR/CIS	4	6
Philippines	4	6
Indonesia	2	2
India	1	1
China	1	1
World	27	47

[1] million instructions per second

SOURCE: Karen Petska Juliussen and Egil Juliussen, 6th Annual Computer Industry Almanac (Lake Tahoe, Calif.: Computer Industry Almanac, Inc., 1993).

sold each year, the fastest-growing market is in programs for personal computers. Word-processing software is the largest seller among these, followed closely by spreadsheet programs, and then by databases and game software.[9]

While the greatest profit margins are now in software, the market for computer hardware is still rapidly expanding. It has, however, become a dog-eat-dog business, with once-fat profit margins rapidly shrinking. Computers and their components have become commodities in highly competitive markets. Many computer manufacturers are finding it difficult to stay in business, and are scrambling for opportunities to cut costs. While the industry—now worth about $315 billion per year worldwide—is still primarily centered in the United States, Japan, and a few other wealthy nations, it has aggressively expanded into developing countries in search of cheap labor. Several newly industrialized countries of the Pacific Rim—including Taiwan, Malaysia, Singapore, and South Korea—have become major producers of computer parts and equipment. A few other developing countries, such as Brazil and India, have substantial—and carefully protected—computer industries which produce primarily for domestic markets.[10]

Computers may soon be more numerous in the United States than cars, which have been perhaps the country's most dominant cultural artifact to date.

The computer sector is distinctively different from traditional heavy industries because the small size and high value of its products make them cheap to ship long distances, and because widespread use of its own products for international communications has given manufacturers the flexibility to locate production and assembly operations far away from their design and management teams. In the structure of its labor force, however, the computer business resembles many older industries. Indeed, the divisions between production workers and those who supervise them and design what they make are probably greater in the computer industry. Small numbers of well-paid executives and technicians supervise much larger numbers of manual laborers, who do the repetitive, less-skilled work of making and assembling components. In the United States, 70 percent of the managers and 60 percent of the professionals are white males. In contrast, only 17 percent of the semi-skilled production workers are white males, while 63 percent are women—of whom half are non-white.[11]

Electronics industry workers are also rarely unionized. In the United States, whereas union members account for more than 50 percent of the steel and automobile workers, 32 percent of those in aircraft manufacturing, 21 percent in petrochemicals, and 17 percent of the country's workers overall, the union membership among electronics workers in recent years has been under 3 percent. Worldwide, electronics manufacturing has strongly resisted unionization. While lack of a union is probably not a problem for the industry's well-paid professional workers—the best of whom often benefit from bidding wars for their services—it leaves production workers without any organized advocacy. This situation, combined with widespread international subcontracting—sometimes to illegal sweatshops or unregulated, household-based pieceworkers—makes it difficult to be certain that any computer, no matter what origin is listed on its label, was produced under decent labor or environmental conditions.[12]

The highly competitive, mobile nature of the computer industry has given it enormous leverage over national governments, communities, and its own workers. This leverage, and its reputation as the industry of the future, have led some communities and countries to bid for its facilities with generous tax breaks and concessions on environmental standards. New Mexico, for example, has offered Intel $2 billion in industrial revenue bond financing, $300 million in tax abatement, the right to pump 6 million gallons per day of scarce desert water, and permits for 350 tons per year of volatile air pollution as incentives for siting a new chip-production facility within the state.[13]

In its overall impacts on the world, the computer is a technological loose cannon—a device with huge capacity to change ecological and economic health for better or worse, whose industry does not yet have its own house in order. Above all, it is an industry that epitomizes the speed with which the conditions of human activity are changing; even as it begins to come to grips with its own social and environmental failures, it is already having profound impacts on how many other human activities are conducted.

Monitoring and Modeling: the Economy and the Biosphere

We understand remarkably little about the planet's ecosystems or the millions of species that make them up. All too often, species vanish forever before they are even identified and named, let alone studied; Harvard biologist Edward O. Wilson has estimated that some 50,000 species are condemned to extinction each year in the tropical rainforests alone, mostly as a result of human activity. At the same time, our understanding of the full impacts of this activity—whether in mining, farming, ranching, or manufacturing—is also minimal. The amounts, effects and fate of many of the thousands of pollutants and synthetic compounds now loosed upon the environment remain largely unknown.[14]

Even as it comes to grips with its own social and environmental failures, the computer industry is profoundly affecting how other human activities are conducted.

Computers offer enormous power for collecting, storing, and organizing information that can help us understand the global environment and our effect on it. Systems for performing these tasks fall into two main categories: monitoring and modeling. Monitoring systems are used to study and keep track of industrial and natural processes—such as the release of carbon dioxide, or the rise in atmospheric temperature. Modeling systems are used to test theories about complex processes, such as the causal relationship *between* carbon dioxide and atmospheric temperature—thereby allowing the simulation of experiments too dangerous or time-consuming to conduct in the "real world."

A form of industrial monitoring in which the United States has made rapid progress is pollution tracking—the identification of what toxic substances are being released, in what quantities, where and by whom. In 1986, American environmentalists fought for and won the Emergency Planning and Right-to-Know Act, which created the world's most comprehensive national pollution database—the Toxics Release Inventory (TRI), which includes data on toxic chemicals released to land, air, and water from about 24,000 U.S. industrial facilities each year.[15]

The TRI was founded on the belief that the residents of communities where industries operate have a right to know the hazards those industries might inflict upon them. When it was first proposed, the inventory was assailed by the Reagan administration and many industry groups as a paperwork nightmare. Indeed, with traditional methods of record-keeping, the system would likely have become just that. Using computers, however, the U.S. Environmental Protection Agency (EPA) and the state pollution agencies, which collect the original forms, have been able to efficiently manage the large amount of data—82,000 reporting forms were filed for 1991, the most recent year for which data are available—and issue national and state reports on a timely basis. Praise for the TRI has even come from some industry leaders, who credit it with raising awareness of their own pollution problems—and helping them save previously wasted chemicals and money.[16]

Public knowledge of pollution problems—and the pressure to clean up that often comes with it—can dramatically change a company's willingness to reduce its emissions. In Northfield, Minnesota, for example, a study of 1987 TRI data by the Natural Resources Defense Council (NRDC) sharply altered the way residents regarded a local manufacturer of electronic circuits. The study revealed that the company, Sheldahl, Inc., was releasing 400 tons of methylene chloride, a suspected carcinogen, into the air each year—enough to rank the facility as the 45th-largest emitter of cancer-causing chemicals in the United States. Community groups brought public pressure to bear on the firm, and worked in concert with Sheldahl employees to negotiate sharp emissions reductions as part of a new union contract.[17]

In other places, as well, public release of TRI data has proved to be a powerful stimulus for industrial cleanup. Grassroots groups around the country have used TRI figures to produce more than 150 reports on local, regional, and national toxic pollution problems. Such studies have repeatedly exposed chronic polluters, putting pressure on them to reform. Their preparation has been made easier by the fact that the inventory is not only compiled in computerized form but can be—and often is—retrieved by outside groups using their own PCs. The Toxics Release Inventory was the first federal database ever required by Congress to be released to the public in a computer-readable format.[18]

For all its usefulness, the TRI could still be improved. It is a limited system, covering only an estimated 5 percent of the United States' total toxic emissions, according to the congressional Office of Technology Assessment. The Community Right-to-Know Act requires facilities to report emissions of only about 300 toxic chemicals. Many other chemicals—including more than 500 regulated as hazardous under other U.S. laws—are not included on the TRI. In addition, only large firms in manufacturing industries—steel, paper, chemicals, petroleum refining, and so on—are required to report. Neither are firms in non-manufacturing industries, including oil and gas extraction, warehousing, transportation, hazardous waste disposal, incineration, and mining. And the accuracy of the reported data is open to question, since they are usually estimates, rather than measured emissions.[19]

Nonetheless, the TRI concept has attracted attention beyond U.S. borders. Canada's National Pollutant Release Inventory system—largely modeled on the TRI—was supposed to begin collecting data in 1993. Early reports indicated that it would also include some pollutants and industries not included in the TRI. As this paper was being written, however, some key issues—including the right of citizens to see the data that companies submit—were still unresolved. Meanwhile, the European Community is considering a toxics reporting system for its 12 nations, with a Brussels conference on the subject scheduled for January 1994. These moves come on the heels of Agenda 21, the blueprint for global environmental cooperation agreed upon by all United Nations members at the 1992 Earth Summit in Rio de Janeiro, which recognized the concept of community right-to-know and recommended that all nations move to establish TRI-style pollution tracking systems.[20]

In addition to providing effective means of storing and retrieving data, computers can speed and simplify their collection. Somewhat surprisingly, for an era in which satellites systematically scan every inch of the globe, a wide variety of environmentally important data are in short supply. For example, a 1992 World Resources Institute study stated "there is no global monitoring of...transboundary [air] pollution flows...ultraviolet radiation, acid precipitation...desertification or land degradation, land conversion, deforestation...ocean productivity, biodiversity, [or] species destruction." The same study summed up the global environmental data situation as "abysmal."[21]

New computerized monitoring techniques provide a means of quickly closing some of these data gaps. Technicians can now make instant assessments of air quality at industrial facilities or hazardous-waste cleanup sites by using handheld sampling devices with built-in disk drives, making it easy to transfer data directly to computers. They need not pause to write down readings, which are automatically recorded along with the date and time. Computers connected to networks of fixed sampling devices can continuously monitor ambient concentrations of pollutants, automatically delivering reports at regular intervals or when an irregularity is detected.[22]

Satellites now yield a continuous flow of information on atmospheric gas concentrations, forest cover, crop health, and other environmental indicators. All of this information is beamed to earth and processed, and can now be viewed in combination with data from other sources. Careful programming is in order, however. In the early 1980s, computers repeatedly threw out satellite readings of extremely low ozone concentrations over the South Pole because they deviated too far from normal expectations. Programmers had assumed that readings so far off the scale would have to be the result of equipment errors. Their oversight delayed detection of the ozone hole for several years.[23]

Monitoring technology can also be used to study biological systems. David Mech of the U.S. Fish and Wildlife Service and his team of field researchers use computerized animal collars equipped with miniature radio transmitters, motion sensors, and sedative darts to study wolf behavior in northern Minnesota. Handheld radio sets allow the researchers to track wolf movements and activity states (the motion sensors reveal whether an animal's head is up or down), as well as to control the collars. A researcher who wishes to examine, inoculate, or relocate an animal simply sends a coded radio signal which ejects a sedative dart from the collar into the animal, immobilizing it.[24]

Biologists—and others interested in their findings—can view their data on animal populations, migrations, breeding sites, and hunting areas in conjunction with land-use information and other data by using geographical information systems (GIS), which both store and organize geographical information and allow it to be quickly displayed in the form of maps. In British Columbia, the Sierra Club of Western Canada is using a GIS to create detailed maps of forest cover on Vancouver Island. The project has revealed that only 23 percent of the island's original low-elevation temperate rainforests—an increasingly endangered ecosystem—remain uncut, and that 82 percent of the island's land is currently allocated to

Computers repeatedly threw out satellite readings of extremely low ozone concentrations over the South Pole because programmers had assumed readings that deviated so far from expectations must be due to equipment errors.

logging. It has also shown that the remaining forest has become increasingly fragmented—further threatening the survival of the ancient ecosystems. The GIS has provided vital information in the Sierra Club's fight to gain government protection for ancient rainforests on the island. Only about 3 percent of such forests are currently protected. Such systems can also provide valuable information to urban planners. Columbus, Ohio, for example, is using a GIS system to design and implement a plan for managing its polluted stormwater runoff—a task required of all large U.S. cities by the Clean Water Act.[25]

Beyond monitoring, computer systems serve a far more ambitious—and potentially critical—function: to model industrial and biological systems. By simulating how those systems might perform under various conditions, the models can show the likely impacts of alternative policies. Perhaps the best-known of these are the global warming models described in the introductory section. Such simulations require powerful supercomputers, because of the thousands of factors that affect climate. Computers are also being used to design a wide variety of products for reduced environmental impacts. Computer modeling of automobile aerodynamics, for instance, has helped bring about increases in the fuel economy of new cars.[26]

On a smaller scale, the computer revolution is changing patterns of personal learning, as well as of institutional research. Popular programs like SimEarth allow computer users to simulate the growth and impacts of entire civilizations. EnviroAccount allows computer users to assess their environmental impacts—and track how changes in lifestyle can change them. And the Global Lab, an international project of the Boston-based Technical Education Research Center, has helped schoolchildren learn about environmental problems by monitoring them themselves. Students use computers to collect data and examine their results, and to share their results—via computer networks—with children in other countries.[27]

Networking for Sustainable Development

In August 1993, the author of this paper typed a note into his computer (in Washington, D.C.) and sent it by electronic mail to a colleague based in Zambia. As it happened, the intended recipient had left Zambia for a visit to England. However, instead of awaiting his return, like a conventional letter, the message was automatically relayed to a computer in England. When the recipient replied, he apologized for his "delayed" response. The entire process had taken 44 hours—less than two days—and the cost was negligible.

With nearly 1.5 million host systems, the Internet now serves an estimated 11 million people.

Experiences like this are commonplace in the world of computer networks. Electronic mail (e-mail) is so fast—a lengthy document can go from London to Sydney in a few hours, or even a few seconds, depending on the system used—that enthusiasts refer to conventional postal service as "snail-mail." E-mail is cheaper than international phone calls, faxes, or express package services, and allows its users to bypass busy signals, unpredictable postal service, and schedule conflicts created by different time zones. The rapidly growing international web of computer systems has made it easy for many people to keep in touch with friends or colleagues on the other side of the world.

Electronic mail and computer conferencing—a form of electronic mail that allows groups of users to share information—have also become vital tools for those who work on environmental and social issues. As of mid-1993, thousands of environmental activists and organizations around the world are using commercial and nonprofit computer networks to coordinate campaigns, exchange news, and get details on the proposals of governments and international organizations. Greenpeace, the world's largest and most far-flung environmental group, has been using its own computer network to coordinate its activities for a decade. Commercial computer systems, such as CompuServe and America Online, offer environmental information sources and online discussions of such issues. The massive Internet—the world's largest collection of computer networks—has extensive resources for environmentalists. And specialized systems, such as Poptel/GeoNet and those of the Association for Progressive Communications (APC)—a group of 10 computer networks—make peace, human rights, labor issues, world development, and the environment their primary focus.[28]

By itself, a computer is a valuable device. But there are limits to the amount of information and the variety of programs that can be assembled on even the largest individual machine. The usefulness of any computer increases dramatically when it is linked to other machines, since networks allow users to pool their resources. A small network—by wiring together all the computers in an office or school, for example—can make it possible to share printers, databases of contacts or clients, or a fax system. Larger networks, which can collect the resources of thousands or millions of users, can be a force for social change.

Large networks put enormous resources and reliable, inexpensive global communications at the fingertips of ordinary citizens. Those with small computers can gain access to the enormous processing power of larger machines. A climate scientist in New York, for example, may develop programs on a small workstation in her own laboratory, and then run them on a supercomputer in California or North Carolina, with the results fed back to her machine. Large computers can be used as repositories for vast quantities of information—library catalogs, the full texts of books and periodicals, or software useful on a wide variety of machines—which can then be reached by any other computer on the network. The author of this paper, for example, obtained numerous articles on networking and the use of computers in developing countries from an archive 5,000 kilometers from his office.[29]

Computer networks are still in their adolescence. While some systems have millions of users, they can still be difficult to use, reflecting their origins as communications tools for computer scientists. And, like local phone systems at the dawn of the telephone age, many networks today are unable to communicate with each other, either because they are not physically connected, or because they are built to different standards.

This situation is changing rapidly, however. The Internet is a fast-growing collection of computer networks that *can* talk to one another. It is beginning to resemble the global phone system in its scope and common design. With nearly 1.5 million host systems—large computers on which many users, who may connect to them by telephone, have accounts—it now serves an estimated 11 million people. Thousands of systems, large and small, are adopting Internet standards every month, bringing multitudes of users into the global web.

E-mail is cheaper than international phone calls, faxes, or express package services—and generally more sure to get through.

Both the number of host computers and the volume of information flowing through the system are estimated to be doubling every five months. Recent new users have included the president and vice president of the United States and a number of U.S. Congressional staff.[30]

The Internet originated in 1969 as a link between computer centers doing defense-related research across the United States. By the late 1980s, it had grown to become an important link for other academic researchers—from English professors to physicists—and had reached outside academia and the borders of the United States. Internet connections now reach into more than 50 countries. The Internet can be difficult to use, and the amount and variety of information available through it can be bewildering. However, many host computers now offer special programs that allow users to search thousands of systems for information on particular topics—without knowledge of special commands or network addresses. The resources available—which include the catalogs of the Library of Congress and many U.S. university libraries, and specialized databases on thousands of subjects—are expanding as rapidly as the system itself. At last count, 135 different journals were being published electronically, and Internet users were discussing a wild variety of topics—from Shakespeare to population growth—via thousands of computer conferences.[31]

These conferences constitute a new and unique form of communication. Functioning like an electronic bulletin board—participants "post" contributions, which are then available for others to read when they log in—they make possible conversations that are lively, global, and immediate. When something significant happens almost anywhere in the world, word of it usually spreads more quickly through computer networks than through other information channels, since there are millions of users and fewer delays than are usually involved in television, radio, or telephone communication. Fans of obscure rock groups can get the latest word on their idols' tours from their counterparts on other continents. Birders and biologists can share information on migrations and rare and endangered species.

There are dozens of Internet mailing lists on environment- and development-related issues, in addition to other environmental resources on the system, such as archives of documents, databases on energy use, and the catalogs of environmental libraries. Internet users can also connect through it to the APC networks, the world's largest assembly of online environmental information and activists. Organized on the model of Econet/Peacenet, its partner network in the United States and the source of the system's common software, the APC also includes networks based in Australia, Brazil, Canada, Ecuador, Germany, Nicaragua, Russia, Sweden, the United Kingdom, and Uruguay. Altogether, the system connects 17,000 activists in 94 countries. And users pay just $3 to $20 per hour, depending on their mode of access and the time of day.[32]

For this price, APC network users can read and participate in nearly a thousand of the system's own conferences on virtually every topic related to the environment, sustainable development, and peace issues, as well as in thousands more conferences from the Internet and other systems. Though the quality and level of participation in the individual conferences varies greatly, the information can be detailed, global, and breathtakingly up-to-date. On a recent day, for example, a glance at a conference on rainforests revealed a news bulletin from Brazil about the murder, discovered three days earlier, of Yanomami Indians in a remote corner of the Amazon basin—a story reported 2-3 days later by U.S. newspapers—and several recent news reports on the struggle of indigenous tribes in Sarawak (Malaysia) for land rights. For those who wanted to find out about a proposed mine in a western Canada wilderness area, or the status of a fight against a new motorway in England, APC conferences provided answers.[33]

APC users can communicate with each other, and with anyone linked to the Internet or other networks, via e-mail. The system proved invaluable during the Russian coup of 1991, when its member network GlasNet—along with RELCOM, another Russian computer network—kept many Russian citizens in contact with each other and the outside world while the military conspirators closed down Russian radio and television news. Western news services monitored conferences on the networks and used them to communicate with sources in the USSR. Computer users in the West relayed outside news reports back to Russian users, who in turn passed them on to their communities.[34]

The Internet is beginning to resemble the global phone system in its scope and design.

The APC networks also played an important role in enabling citizen participation before and during the June, 1992 United Nations Conference on Environment and Development (UNCED), held in Rio de Janeiro, Brazil. Preparatory and draft conference documents entered the system starting in late 1990, and final versions were made available at the end of the conference. APC's Brazilian member network, Alternex, set up temporary computer facilities in Rio for users who were attending the U.N. meeting and the related gathering for non-governmental organizations (NGOs). This made it easy for the various NGO representatives to report back to their offices on the progress of the meeting, work out lobbying positions, and communicate with the press back home.[35]

The electronic mail service provided by international computer networks can help international organizations share information and keep track of their far-flung activities. For instance, ICEF, the Brussels-based international union representing workers in chemical and related industries, makes extensive use of e-mail to communicate with about 30 of its member unions around the world. The unions communicate primarily through the Poptel system of GeoNet, a public-interest computer network based in Western Europe. ICEF research director Jim Catterson and his small staff responded to 1,756 electronic requests for information in 1992—without ever going to a library. Instead, using commercial database systems such as Data-Star, Dialog, and Pergamon Information as his primary sources, he can provide his members with occupational health and safety data, as well as financial and corporate strategy information on individual companies. Such background information can be invaluable to national unions negotiating contracts or health and safety policies, or contemplating strikes. Catterson notes that in years past the unions could not communicate quickly enough to coordinate international action against individual companies. Organizers now often find that companies' internal communications systems are not as quick as those of the unions.[36]

Greenpeace uses its computer network to monitor international traffic in hazardous waste. Campaigners stay in virtually hourly contact, exchanging information about movements of waste by ship, train, and truck. They used the system in 1988 to spread the word about a large toxic waste dump found in the Nigerian village of Koko, and the waste's effects on the health of local citizens. During the ensuing international uproar, the waste was traced back to an Italian company, and environmentalists successfully called for an international conference on trade in such wastes. The same campaigners recently discovered that large amounts of lead- and cadmium-laced wastes were being shipped from the United States to Bangladesh, where they were sold as fertilizer.[37]

Networks can also allow people to sift through large collections of environmental data for the information they need.

Michael Stein, a San Francisco-based writer and network expert who has been closely involved with Econet and its affiliates for years, believes that access to databases eventually will prove to be one of the most important services of environmental computer networks. Econet/Peacenet, the APC's U.S. affiliate, makes available a variety of useful databases, including the EPA and other library catalogs, a database of environmental funding sources, and one that lists fax numbers for various world leaders, press organizations, and every member of the U.S. Congress. The Washington-based International Institute for Energy Conservation provides Econet/Peacenet users with InfoTree, a database of articles, institutions, and other information on energy-efficient technologies and policies. Users of the database can discuss their efforts with others through an accompanying conference.[38]

A glance revealed a bulletin on the murder of Yanomami Indians in a remote part of the Amazon—a story reported 2 to 3 days later by U.S. news media.

The Right-to-Know Computer Network (RTK Net), based in Washington, D.C. is an excellent example of a public computer network that offers electronic access to useful data. The network is jointly operated by two nonprofit groups, OMB Watch and the Unison Institute. It offers its more than 800 users online access to the U.S. government's TRI database on industrial releases of toxic chemicals. They can combine the information with other government environmental databases—such as those on Superfund hazardous waste cleanup sites and pending environmental litigation—and a variety of census data, including the ethnic and economic characteristics of the local population.[39]

RTK Net was created because the federal government was not making TRI data available online at low or no cost. The same data are available on a federal system—Toxnet, administered by the National Library of Medicine in Bethesda, Maryland—but at a cost of $18 to $20 per hour, which few community-based activists can afford. The federal system is also more difficult to use, and lacks RTK Net's on-line community of activists, who freely share tips on how to conduct searches and spiritedly debate a variety of topics, including environmental racism and the health effects of toxics. Now that a new presidential administration—one more sympathetic to the public dissemination of environmental data—is in office, RTK Net is likely to provide a model for how to make public information electronically accessible. And the system's user pool is likely to expand sharply in the near future, as it is about to become available on the Internet (users will still need to obtain individual accounts).[40]

RTK Net users have generated a large share of the growing stack of TRI-derived reports on U.S. toxic pollution, generating press coverage and public attention and spurring industry cleanup efforts. The ability to combine pollution information with other types of data has resulted in some particularly compelling studies. For example, Florence Robinson of the North Baton Rouge Environmental Association, a community group, has been using RTK Net's TRI data and census information to demonstrate that Louisiana's minority communities live with disproportionately high levels of toxic pollution. She has reported her findings in a series of papers and testified on the subject at a U.S. Civil Rights Commission hearing on environmental racism.[41]

Activists and the general public can also find environmental data on commercial electronic services. The information available on less-expensive commercial systems such as CompuServe and America Online tends to be more general than that available on specialized networks such as Econet. Larger systems—such as U.S.-based Dialog and Nexis, and DataStar in Europe—provide access to hundreds of bibliographic databases in virtually any subject area, as well as full-text access to stories in a variety of prominent newspapers, news services, and specialized journals, but they are quite expensive. At prices that can exceed $80 per hour, they cater primarily to businesses or large organizations.[42]

For those without access to networks, databases and other environmental information are available on computer disks. The World Bank, the World Resources Institute, and Worldwatch

Institute all now provide some of their data on floppy disks. The GreenDisk, a Washington-based "paperless environmental journal," provides on floppy disk the full text of dozens of environmental reports and articles in its six issues per year. And census, transportation and other data are increasingly available on CD-ROMs, laser disks—identical to audio compact disks—that can store thousands of pages of text or large amounts of other data.[43]

Computers and Developing Countries

A t first glance, computer technology might seem of little consequence for the more than three billion people who live in developing countries. Those nations produce very few computers themselves, and usually suffer from chronic shortages of foreign exchange for importing them. They are generally lacking in computer-literate office workers, programmers, service technicians, or spare parts. Their antiquated, overburdened, and sometimes nonexistent telephone and electric power systems and otherwise-inadequate infrastructure can pose substantial obstacles to operating computers and linking them into networks.

Nevertheless, when these problems can be surmounted, the potential benefits of computer use in developing countries are enormous. Computers can be an extraordinary tool for the fight against the two great interconnected problems of Third World development—poverty and environmental degradation. Without computers, residents of developing countries risk becoming even more marginalized within the rapidly evolving world economy. With them, they can communicate with each

Computers can be an extraordinary tool for the fight against the two great interconnected problems of Third World development— poverty and environmental degradation.

other and gain broad access to essential information from around the world. Computer networks can relay the information—protocols for medical treatment, weather reports and crop market information, potential sources of funding—that health professionals, farmers, development workers, and others need to do their jobs better. Networks can link those in even the remotest areas to the global information system, allowing them to send and receive messages as fast as or faster than by other methods—and usually more cheaply. Word-processing, spreadsheet, and database programs can help them manipulate, manage, and understand the wide variety of information that computers and networks make accessible.

Computers can also be a powerful force for democracy—which is a primary determinant of economic productivity. Boston University professor and development writer Sheldon Annis observes that computer networks are now bringing access to information and new channels of communication to Latin America's poor. While the poor do not own computers and modems themselves, says Annis, they increasingly belong to organizations that do. And with computers and other communications tools, those organizations are enabling the poor to participate actively in policy decisions that affect their lives—whereas before they were often ignored by governments and wealthy elites.[44]

Although computers are far less numerous there than in the countries of the Organization for Economic Cooperation and Development (OECD), computer networks already reach into the Third World, Eastern Europe, and the former Soviet Union. A few Internet and Bitnet connections reach academic institutions in such countries—particularly in Eastern Europe, where universities often already have sophisticated computer systems and a reserve of technical specialists—giving them access to those systems' enormous wealth of files, services, and fellow users. In Latin America and the Caribbean, the Organization of American States launched its Hemisphere-Wide Networking Initiative in 1991 to foster the interconnection of academic computer systems throughout the region. Such systems are technically complicated, however, and require costly, high-quality telecommunications lines. As a result, in most Third World areas, they are not available. In particular, they are almost nonexistent in sub-Saharan Africa, with the exception of South Africa. Even where they do exist, the academic networks rarely reach outside of big cities—and primarily serve an affluent, well-educated pool of users.[45]

Luckily, there are other alternatives. The APC networks, for example, reach into dozens of Third World countries. While they offer somewhat less technically sophisticated systems and services than the academic networks—primarily conferencing and electronic mail—they provide valuable connections between non-governmental organizations and activists working on environmental and development issues. In Brazil, for example, Alternex ties together 826 different organizations located throughout the country, including some in remote areas of the Amazon Basin. Nicarao has connected Nicaraguan activists with each other and the outside world since 1989, and now boasts 385 users. In Bolivia, Uruguay, and Ecuador, similar services are now provided by Bolnet, Chasque, and Ecuanex. And since all the APC networks are tied closely together, their conferences reach far across borders and continents.[46]

Without computers, residents of developing countries risk becoming even more marginalized within the rapidly evolving world economy.

The RIO Network—a project of ORSTOM, a French public research institute—has 800 users in France and a dozen tropical developing countries in Africa, the South Pacific, and the Caribbean, with connections to six countries more planned for 1993. Originally designed to link researchers working on ORSTOM-related projects, the network now serves other scientists and non-governmental organizations working on development. The network is technologically sophisticated, linking a mix of high-powered scientific workstations and personal computers.[47]

Third World computers can also gain access to the worldwide

web of electronic networks through a grassroots networking program called FidoNet, developed by U.S. computer hobbyists. FidoNet is a low-cost method of linking together computer bulletin board systems through ordinary phone lines. Its virtue—and its usefulness in developing countries—lies in its ability to overcome the limitations of inadequate phone systems. FidoNet systems automatically contact each other at night—when phone rates are low—to exchange conference postings and electronic mail messages. They keep dialing until they make a connection, and do not stop transmitting until assured by the machine at the other end that all messages have been received free of errors. Regular connections, called gateways, between FidoNet computers and other systems such as the Internet and the APC networks, allow FidoNet users to communicate with virtually anyone with an electronic mail address, with most messages reaching their destination within 24 hours.[48]

FidoNet computers can even operate where no telephone system exists, by using a technique called "packet radio." Packet radio sets—small devices with simple antennas—are attached to a computer much like a modem, and can be used to exchange electronic mail and other data automatically. In areas where the computers are separated by long distances, packet radio sets can transmit their messages via low-orbit satellites, which—as they pass overhead—then relay the information to other computers. Motorola is now developing a system of 77 such satellites that, when completed, will provide continuous coverage everywhere on earth.[49]

Such technology is being used to get valuable information into the hands of people in remote areas who need it. SatelLife, a Boston-based nonprofit organization, uses low-orbit satellites and electronic mail to distribute medical information in sub-Saharan Africa. The Boston office has an account on Peacenet, which it uses to communicate with its African staff and clients with FidoNet connections. The system's primary users are doctors at African universities, who can receive *New England Journal of Medicine* articles free of charge, as well as other medical information. Similarly, Volunteers in Technical Assistance (VITA) uses FidoNet connections and packet radio to link its small-business development projects in two cities in Chad with its headquarters in Arlington, Virginia.[50]

As mentioned earlier, however, there are a variety of obstacles to such programs—including a lack of computers in the developing world, and the expense of importing new machines. Apple and other manufacturers have created donation programs to get new machines to deserving organizations, but the recipients have usually been educational institutions or nonprofit groups in industrialized countries. Another solution is for users in the industrialized countries, where computers are quickly outmoded, to pass them on to Third World users who would be delighted to have them. While Internet and other high-technology computer networks require powerful machines, even some old, outmoded personal computers can run FidoNet programs, providing a communications link that is as fast as a telex—at a fraction of the cost.[51]

Motorola is now developing a system of 77 satellites that will provide continuous coverage everywhere on earth.

One of the greatest values of computers in the Third World is their ability to function without reliable infrastructure—not only without telephones, but without reliable electricity. In developing countries, power is often not available—and when it is, it may go on and off unpredictably, or vary substantially in frequency or voltage. Lights and other basic electrical devices are often not terribly sensitive to such fluctuations, but computers and other sophisticated electronic devices are. Even slight variations in power supply can damage a computer or interrupt its normal operation. Such problems can be avoided, however, with a widely available device that isolates a machine from the outlet power and provides hours—or days, if necessary—of battery power in case the main power fails. Such "uninterruptible power supplies" are available for as little as $200. Portable computers, which now may be as small as a notebook, can do the same thing; since they are usually designed to be run on rechargeable batteries and used in different countries, they can handle widely varying supplies of electricity. And in rural areas where grid power does not exist, solar or wind power installations are becoming increasingly available.[52]

Software is also often a problem for Third World computer users. Legitimate copies of basic programs are often difficult to obtain, and, if they can be found, are usually very expensive. Even in the U.S. market, sophisticated word-processing, spreadsheet, or database programs have until recently typically cost $400 to $500. Recent heavy competition has brought prices down somewhat—in some cases to less than $100—but such prices are still prohibitive for hundreds of millions of people. As a result, most software used in developing countries is pirated—illegally copied—rather than purchased from the firm that produced it. Instruction manuals are rarely available, and even if the software maker offers local support services—a rare situation in developing countries—they are not usually available to those who cannot prove they acquired the software legitimately.[53]

Additional problems accrue from the fact that most software is written in the United States for the U.S. market—and the rest is created mainly in other wealthy, industrialized countries for local use. As a result, virtually no programs are available in indigenous languages. This is less of a problem in countries where colonial languages are pervasively used—in much of Latin America, for example—than in places where tribal languages still predominate, including large parts of Africa and Asia. The lack of software in local languages can reinforce existing inequities, limiting the pool of computer users to those who are fluent in the country's colonial language or other foreign languages.[54]

If planners or funders of Third World computer systems fail to take software needs into account, their investments can be rendered useless. Third World observers often report that expensive, sophisticated computers donated by aid organizations or development institutions sit idle because of inappropriate, undocumented, or improperly installed software—or simply because no one in the local organization or area has the expertise to solve even basic problems. The lack of local education and training in the software can leave local non-governmental human rights, health, or environmental organizations completely dependent on the expertise of expatriates. And the lack of trained local personnel makes it even harder to retain those that are trained; NGOs often find that once they have become computer-literate, local staff members leave quickly for private-sector jobs.[55]

A variety of programs can help give residents of developing countries access to the growing web of computerized information. Particularly important are efforts to funnel both new and used computers—properly equipped for local conditions—into the Third World. The programs also need to provide sufficient access to repairs, spare parts, and technical advice—and assistance with the development of networks. Such programs should promote not only high-quality academic networks, but also low-cost systems, such as FidoNet, that can surmount infrastructure problems and reach far outside developed areas. Local and satellite packet-radio services can help extend the reach of such systems when telephone systems are inadequate.

Expensive computers donated by aid organizations often sit idle for lack of adequate software or expertise.

Several levels of solutions are in order for problems with software and computer maintenance in developing countries. One of the highest priorities is to establish international programs to make dependable software, manuals, and support available to NGOs and others at no cost or low cost. These programs should include a major training component, so that local personnel gain the skills necessary to keep systems running over the long run—after the foreign consultants leave for their home countries. Programs for software donation—where the license of old software is actually transferred from the original user to the new group—are also needed.

Unfortunately, the amount of old software available may be declining, as software companies increasingly sell upgrades to existing programs, rather than completely new ones. A needed solution is for software companies to offer their products—and support or manuals for them—at low cost to users in developing countries. This may be an unlikely scenario with new, expensive programs, but companies may be willing to do so with older, still serviceable, software. Such programs are also likely to have fewer (unknown) bugs, since they have been in use for longer.

Finally, there is a pressing need to develop basic computer education programs in Third World schools and universities, so that such countries can build pools of programmers versed in both software and local languages and customs. Local programmers could then modify and adapt foreign programs for local needs. For example, using software originally developed for Roman-alphabet languages where another alphabet prevails requires additional programming to make the keyboard usable. A few developing countries—particularly Brazil and India, which produce computers themselves—possess nascent software industries. India, with its large complement of educated English speakers, is now attracting subcontracted programming work from U.S. software makers. And basic literacy is a prerequisite for computer use. You can't type if you can't read.

The Toxic Price of the Microchip

Computers have always been viewed as "clean." Film, TV, and press images from the industry's early years portray computers in spotless laboratories operated by clean-cut men in white coats. The computer's basic components—first the tube, then the transistor and the microchip—were seen as fundamentally different and more sophisticated than the technologies that made earlier, "dirty" industries possible. Steel mills and chemical plants had belching smokestacks and gas flares that lit the night with noxious colors. Microprocessors, by contrast, were made in "clean rooms," where even the smallest particles of dust were continuously filtered from the air so they would not contaminate the tiny chips.[56]

In reality, computer production is not as clean as the industry's verdant office parks would seem to suggest. The electronics industry uses a large number of toxic or environmentally hazardous substances, many of which escape into workspaces and the environment. While the air in "clean rooms" may be dust-free, it is still often contaminated with hazardous chemical vapors. And the bucolic lawns surrounding semiconductor manufacturers often conceal seriously contaminated land and groundwater.

The most startling contradiction of the notion that computer manufacturing is a "clean" industry is to be found in Santa Clara County, California. Once known mainly for the fruit of its extensive orchards, the county underwent a transformation in the 1970s, becoming the birthplace and center of the booming computer industry, and coming to be known as the now-famous Silicon Valley. Not so well known is that this valley now contains the largest concentration of hazardous-waste cleanup sites in the United States. Much of its groundwater is now contaminated with trichloroethylene (TCE) and 1,1,1-trichloroethane—both chemicals linked to serious health problems—and with a variety of other chemicals used to manufacture and clean electronic components. At least 150 different sites in the area are now being examined or monitored by state, federal, or local authorities; 23 of them are now on the EPA's Superfund list of the nation's most hazardous toxic dumps.[57]

Silicon Valley now contains the largest concentration of hazardous-waste cleanup sites in the United States.

The electronics industry long benefited from a presumption that its activities were environmentally benign. In Silicon Valley, where this industry had become a dominant economic force by the early 1970s, little attention was paid to environmental conditions until 1982, when a leak of toxic solvents from an underground tank at a Fairchild Semiconductor plant was shown to be contaminating the local groundwater and a public water supply well. The ensuing publicity led to the discovery of similar problems at scores of other locations in the area. Since then, millions of dollars have been spent in attempts to clean up some sites, but with only limited success. Some of the chemicals, such as TCE, are virtually impossible to remove completely once they have settled into an aquifer. At some sites, contamination is still uncontrolled and spreading.[58]

At least since 1979, government and public interest groups have suspected that ethylene glycol ethers—solvents commonly used in chip making—could cause reproductive health problems. Indeed, a high incidence of such problems found among some computer industry workers has been clearly linked to their exposure to toxic substances. By 1986, a Digital Equipment Corporation study had found increased miscarriage rates among workers in its Hudson, Massachusetts semiconductor factory. In late 1992, two studies, by IBM and the Semiconductor Industry Association, identified glycol ethers as the cause of high rates of worker miscarriages. And while conclusive data are lacking, epidemiologic studies and a variety of informal reports suggest that water pollution from electronics firms may be causing more widespread health problems, as well. A 1985 California Department of Health Services study, for example, revealed that nearby residents exposed to water contaminated by the Fairchild leak were suffering from two to three times as many miscarriages and birth defects as the general population.[59]

Environmental problems have been found in most of the electronics industry manufacturing areas where researchers have looked. In Phoenix, Arizona—a desert community where drinking water is at a premium—a large plume of TCE has spread through the city's primary aquifer. A Motorola chip-production facility is believed to be the source of much of the contamination. Similar problems exist among the many electronics facilities near Boston, Massachusetts, and at other U.S. sites. And the problems are not limited to the United States. In Japan, where nearly half of the world's semiconductors are made, the industry is believed to be a major cause of extensive groundwater pollution. In South Korea, a toxic form of phenol leaked in April 1991 from a storage tank at an electronics plant into a public water supply serving 1.7 million people. The incident led to large street demonstrations by protesting citizens. It is likely that such problems also exist in Malaysia, Singapore, and other newly industrializing areas where the electronics industry operates.[60]

In the United States, the electronics industry has taken steps to reduce the risk of environmental contamination and worker exposures to hazardous substances. Digital, for example, eliminated ethylene glycol ethers from its semiconductor manufacturing processes by early 1990. Other companies have moved much more slowly, prompting bitter complaints from labor and environmental activists. Only since the 1992 studies have most other firms—including IBM and many other members of the Semiconductor Industry Association—formally warned their workers of hazards from the chemicals, although some had already taken actions to significantly reduce their use.[61]

Those exposed to water contaminated by the leak were suffering from two to three times as many miscarriages and birth defects as the general population.

It is unlikely that much attention would have been devoted to the environmental impacts of electronics industry pollution without continuing crusades by public-interest groups. In the computer industry's heartland, a local activist group, the Silicon Valley Toxics Coalition (SVTC), has played a crucial role in the debate over the impacts of electronics production since the early 1980s. When it was formed, SVTC was a somewhat unusual (for the United States) combination of community, environmental and labor activists. Its membership is ethnically diverse, since minorities and lower-income citizens are disproportionately represented among both the work force and the neighbors of Silicon Valley's electronics facilities. SVTC has fought for proper environmental safeguards and reduced use of toxics in electronics facilities, and was principally responsible for the passage of tough local ordinances regulating the industry. In conjunction with a local labor organization—the Santa Clara Center for Occupational Safety and Health—SVTC has also raised important questions about the industry's disproportionate impact on women and minorities, and the lack of union representation for most electronics workers.[62]

Building on SVTC's example, groups in other U.S. communities with major electronics facilities are now actively campaigning on the same issues. They include, among others, the Southwest Organizing Project, based in Albuquerque, New Mexico, and the Austin, Texas-based People Organized in Defense of Earth and its Resources (PODER). Such groups have joined together with SVTC in a coalition—the Campaign for Responsible Technology—to raise such issues at a national level. The coalition scored a major victory in 1992, when it persuaded Congress to allocate a tenth of the federal contribution to SEMATECH—a government/industry consortium that develops U.S. chip-making technology—for the development of environmentally sound microprocessor production processes. The SEMATECH effort should set important precedents, since it is now being held up as a model for clean technology development projects in a variety of other U.S. industries, as the Clinton administration moves the United States toward a more explicit, civilian-oriented industrial policy.[63]

The potential for success of electronics-industry cleanup efforts is illustrated by the same companies' experience with reducing the use of chlorofluorocarbons (CFCs), the ubiquitous chemicals primarily responsible for the depletion of the stratospheric ozone layer. When it was first suggested that the industry—one of the largest users of CFCs—might have to dramatically reduce or eliminate their use, many companies protested that they were irreplaceable. However, when the U.S. government—in accord with international agreements on ozone depletion—required electronics firms to cut their CFC use, the industry rapidly came up with substitutes. In one well-known case, IBM found a particularly easy substitute for CFCs in one of its manufacturing operations. The simpler alternative—soap and water—was also cheaper. The U.S. electronics industry now expects to eliminate most CFCs from its operations by early 1994.[64]

Cleaning up the electronics industry will require better environmental regulations wherever it operates, as well as enlightened trade rules, given the industry's global nature. The inclusion of labor and community groups in its efforts to reduce environmental and health problems could also help. The CRT and other groups have met recently with SEMATECH officials to recommend priorities for research. And beyond SEMATECH, electronics firms and professional associations have already initiated a number of cooperative projects aimed at cleaner production. The Institute of Electrical and Electronics Engineers devoted a large conference to environmental issues in mid-1993. The Microelectronics and Computer Technology Corporation (MCC)—a research consortium supported by about 80 firms—assembled seven industry-wide task forces in 1992 to examine a variety of computer-related environmental issues. They recently published a 350-page report of their findings, which included a recommendation that the industry move toward "green design": crafting their products—and the processes by which they are made—for minimum environmental impact. MCC is now working with the industry to establish a national initiative to address environmental issues. If the industry takes its own recommendations seriously, the prospects for improving its environmental performance should be very good. Few sectors are as accustomed to rapid technical change as the computer industry, where products often become outmoded within months of their debut.[65]

The Environmental Consequences of Computerization

Computers have not always reduced the environmental impacts of those who use them, either. Far from creating a "paperless office," for example—as some early, breathless descriptions of a computerized future forecasted—computers and high-speed printers have enabled office workers to routinely use more paper than they did before such machines were invented. And taken together, these machines use substantial quantities of energy. In the United States, where they are ubiquitous, computers now account for an estimated 5 percent of the commercial electricity load—and constitute its fastest-growing segment. According to the EPA, computers' share could reach 10 percent by the year 2000. Moreover, when computers are thrown away, their toxic components can pose environmental problems if not carefully handled. But strategies are available for mitigating all of these impacts.[66]

Paper use may be the impact most obvious to users. While early expectations were that computers would virtually eliminate the need for paper copies of documents, it turned out that few users were willing to rely solely on electronic storage. Instead, fast, automatic printers and word-processing and desktop-publishing programs have made it possible for people to generate paper documents faster than they ever could with typewriters— encouraging the production of larger numbers of drafts and copies. One very conservative estimate puts the current annual paper consumption by the world's personal computers at 230 million reams, or 115 billion individual sheets.[67]

A few small changes in equipment and behavior could sharply cut the amount of paper used. For instance, most word-processing programs now allow those with laser printers to fit more words on a page by printing in smaller, but still readable, type, and by using narrower margins. Similarly, using a "printing" rather than "typewriting" typeface can substantially cut paper use. A typewriter face uses equal amounts of space for all letters of the alphabet—each small "i" or "t" taking as much as a capital "W", for example—whereas printing typefaces may use only a third as much space for an "i," while being at least equally readable. Laser-printer manufacturers are also beginning to offer two-sided printing, which has long been a common feature in copiers using virtually the same technology. A combination of these measures could cut certain types of paper use by three-fourths.

In the long run, however, paper use will be most dramatically reduced when people routinely choose not to print documents. In certain applications, paper documents are already being phased out. For instance, more than 18,000 U.S. organizations already save paper and postage—and speed their transactions—

by exchanging purchase orders, invoices, and other standard business information in a standardized electronic format called EDI (Electronic Data Interchange). Much more paper could be saved if most of the documents now prepared or recalled on computer screens—from letters to books and articles—were not printed out by those wishing to read them.[68]

Such restraint is not likely until viewing computerized documents is as easy as picking up a book or a magazine. But rapid recent progress in monitor technology and miniature computers suggests that we may soon see the development of a lightweight, book-sized reading device that displays high-resolution, full-color text and graphics. Source material—books, magazines, drafts of work in progress—could be provided on small memory cards, or via easy, plug-in connections with computers. Pages could be "turned" by simply touching the screen or buttons on the reading device. Such a device could probably be produced with existing technology, but most likely would be quite expensive. The price could drop rapidly, however; it is instructive to remember that just a few years ago, the powerful, notebook-sized portable computers now coming to dominate personal computer sales did not exist at all—but now they are widely affordable.

In the long run, paper use will be most dramatically reduced when people routinely choose not to print documents.

In addition to becoming far less paper-hungry, computers can be modifed to consume substantially less energy. A typical machine uses 80 to 160 watts of power, about as much as an incandescent light bulb. Worldwide, computers consume an estimated 240 billion kilowatt-hours of electricity each year—about as much as the entire annual use of Brazil. That, of course, represents a not-insignificant share of total greenhouse emissions.[69]

Only a small fraction of this electricity now powers machines in active use. Most computers are left on all day, even while their users take phone calls, meet, file, or go to lunch. Thirty to forty percent of computers are even left running at night and on weekends.   Most current machines don't turn on quickly, so many users prefer to keep them always at the ready. Many people have as much trouble remembering to turn off their computers as they do remembering to turn off the lights.[70]

The answer to these human failings is to develop machines that automatically drop into a low power-consumption state— in effect, go to sleep—when not in use, yet wake up immediately when needed. Computer makers have already developed low-power computer technology for another segment of their market—notebook-sized portable machines. Limited by the low electrical storage capacity of existing batteries, designers of portable machines have made their systems highly energy-efficient. Virtually all such machines now feature an automatic sleep mode.

To encourage computer makers to design such features into all their equipment, the U.S. EPA launched its Energy Star Computers program in June 1992. The program is a cooperative venture between the agency and leading computer and monitor makers, who have agreed to improve the energy efficiency of their desktop equipment. If their products meet Energy Star's power-saving standards, which require computers or monitors to be able to drop into a sleep mode of 30 watts or less, the firms are entitled to use a special logo on their products and in advertising. The first Energy Star products were released in June 1993, and as of August, 89 computer companies, 19 printer producers, and 39 component and software makers had signed up for the program. The participating computer and printer companies account, respectively, for 70 and 90 percent of sales in their industries. Participating firms say that most of their products should meet Energy Star guidelines within a year or two, and that the added efficiency should not affect their performance or price.[71]

Happily for the Energy Star participants, the EPA is working to build a substantial market for energy-efficient computers. It is coordinating with the General Services Administration (the agency that buys or approves the purchase of most federal office equipment), the Department of Energy, and other federal agencies to encourage the purchase of Energy Star products. The

U.S. government, which spends $4 billion per year on computer equipment, is the industry's largest customer. EPA is also rounding up commitments from businesses, estimating that the program should save up to $1 billion worth of electricity each year—enough to power all of Vermont and New Hampshire. A synergistic benefit is that sleeping computers will emit much less heat, thus reducing the energy needed for cooling office buildings. If Energy Star products capture two-thirds of the market by the year 2000, their use could prevent 20 million tons of carbon dioxide from pouring out of electric power plants each year—an amount equal to the output of 5 million automobiles, or the total number of new cars produced in the United States each year. Also kept out of the air will be thousands of tons of nitrogen and sulfur oxides—the principal causes of acid rain.[72]

> **"Sleeping" computers could reduce CO_2 emissions by 20 million tons in the United States— equal to the output of 5 million cars.**

Other aspects of computer design are also important in determining the machines' lifetime impacts on the environment. The Microelectronics and Computer Technology Corporation study included an assessment of the overall life-cycle impacts of a model computer workstation. In addition to energy efficiency, it identified the use of recycled materials, ease of disassembly and reuse, the use of low-toxicity materials, and reduced product packaging as important design features.[73]

The software industry, too, is beginning to examine the impacts of producing and disposing of its packaging and products—including voluminous software manuals that immediately become outdated upon the release of new program versions. The growing availability and falling price of drives that can read CD-ROMs, which hold thousands of pages of information, should help alleviate the need for paper manuals. Already, many programs include such extensive on-line help systems that manuals are rarely used. CD-ROMs could also help reduce the number of floppy disks needed (there are now billions in use, an unknown number of which are thrown away each year). Discards could also be reduced by reuse; a company in Washington state has recently begun recovering thousands of used disks, reformatting and testing them, and packaging them for resale.[74]

In Europe, the long-term fate of computers has become a major issue. Germany is developing an ordinance requiring manufacturers of all electronic consumer goods—including radios, televisions, and computers—to take back their products at the end of their useful lives. This is likely to compel manufacturers to design computer components for upgradeability or reuse whenever possible. The ordinance is scheduled to take effect in early 1994, with its most restrictive provisions likely to be phased in over several years.[75]

Somewhat surprisingly, it now seems clear that there should be very little need to actually dispose of computers. Computers rarely wear out; they are usually discarded because their users regard them as obsolete. But old machines can still be valuable to users who cannot afford new ones. Schools and community groups are often overjoyed to receive donated equipment, and many local programs now facilitate such exchanges. And even machines that seem completely outdated can be highly prized in countries where computers are rare.

Since 1990, the East-West Educational Development Foundation in Boston, Massachusetts has funneled thousands of donated personal computers to universities, non-governmental organizations, and journalists in Eastern Europe and the former Soviet Union. The group tests donated machines, repairs them when necessary, and identifies potential recipients. In 1992, it identified 200 times as much need for computers as it could satisfy. A similar program was set up in the United Kingdom, in 1993, by the Science, Technology and Development Forum, a charitable group which also coordinates the donation of technical literature to institutions in developing countries. An institution in Cambodia was the first recipient of donated computers, and the group plans to send machines to recipients in Zambia in the near future.[76]

Computers can also have physical effects on those who use them. Thousands of people now suffer from carpal tunnel syndrome—a painful wrist inflammation—and other injuries linked to long hours working at computer keyboards. Staring at a computer screen for long hours can cause vision problems, and magnetic fields from video display terminals are also a suspected cause of reproductive problems. Sustainable working hours for those who use computer terminals could help alleviate or avoid some such problems. Technological change is the ultimate solution, however: voice recognition programs and equipment could eventually eliminate the need to type, and newer types of display terminals—such as the liquid crystal screens now common on portable computers—do not put out strong magnetic fields.[77]

Computers and Global Thinking

From the beginning, humans have been tool-makers. And since we first sharpened sticks and stones into spears and knives, human technological development has been driven almost completely by the desire to expand our dominion over nature—and each other. The significance of any tool lies not in its technological wizardry, but in how we use it. While our tools have become enormously sophisticated, our use of them often has not—and the consequences are all around us, in devastated ecosystems and impoverished people.

Are computers any different from the technologies that preceded them? It is certainly possible to view them in the same light. Indeed, their principal uses in the first several decades of their existence were military, bureaucratic, and commercial. The first program run on the first computer was used to help design the hydrogen bomb, and computer guidance systems have made intercontinental ballistic missiles—and the possibility of global thermonuclear war—a reality. Computers are widely used by governments and corporations to track our credit records, our tastes in music, food, and sex, and our political opinions—and to target them for the next election or advertising campaign. There is ample possibility that the use of these machines will simply prime the pump of consumer economies, accelerating the relentless assault of modern industry on the planet's resources and peoples, while exacerbating existing social inequities.

But computers also have the potential to serve a fundamentally different purpose: extending human understanding of the environment—and our own activities—to the point where we can fulfill René Dubos' famous dictum to "think globally." Computers will not provide us with all the answers to our global problems: they are simply machines—extremely precise and lightning fast, but not very bright—that do only what we tell them to do. They can, however, give us global eyes and ears in an age where our actions often have worldwide impacts.

Global thinking is a tall order: human beings are not naturally built for it. To achieve it, we need tools that extend our senses, and that enhance our ability to comprehend the information they collect. Computers can make up for the natural limits to our view of the world by helping us convert unintelligible masses of data into forms we understand. Sifting through pages of raw data on even the most fascinating subject can be a stultifying experience, but the same data converted into graphs, charts, or enhanced photographs can grab our attention, because they allow us to use the same visual skills that make it possible for us—miraculously—to pick out a familiar face in a crowded room.

Computers have become useful, personal devices because a few visionaries among their early developers dared to believe they could be something more than inscrutable, centralized tools operated by experts for large institutions. The machines are continuing to evolve toward forms that will allow us to communicate with them—and get back answers—in forms that appeal to all our senses, making the most of our powerful *human* ability to recognize patterns by sight, sound, and touch. The metal boxes with keyboards and screens that we now think of as computers may well disappear, as the microprocessors at their heart are integrated with other devices. No longer will people have to learn to think like computers; computers will instead be programmed to communicate like people. Working with a computer may become more like talking to a television that talks back—and that can quickly search the world for the information one needs.

The same kind of vision is needed as we develop the extensive computer networks—the "information highways" of popular discussion—that will soon link much of the world. Those networks have the potential to bring all of us—rich and poor, rural and urban—the information we need to make the difficult choices required for the creation of a sustainable society. But without careful attention to the public policies that govern their evolution and application, they are unlikely to be a force for reducing the environmental impacts of industrial civilization, ending poverty, and strengthening participatory democracy. Particularly important is that they become easy to use and accessible to all, and that governments take steps to make a wide range of public information—from industrial pollution data to health and census information—easily and cheaply available through them.

Whether they are used to rebuild the world's economy or simply to drive it mindlessly faster, the most intriguing fact about computers is that they vastly increase our ability to control. In this, they have so far followed the pattern of all human history, as each new technology has been turned by its users to the control of nature or other people, rather than of their own increasingly unsustainable behavior. It would be an all-too-predictable mistake to use the computer as simply a new, more effective way for us to dominate our world. We have another choice: computers can help us learn to live with nature. Rather than our machines controlling us, we can begin to control them—and ourselves.

Notes

Note on electronic sources:

Many of the references for this paper were obtained on-line. When possible, both on-line and print versions of documents are cited. APC conferences, which the author reached via Econet—the APC's U.S. system—are listed by name in brackets. Electronic mail addresses and ftp addresses (for documents obtained by Internet remote file transfer) are listed similarly. An excellent overview of the Internet, its information resources, and how to reach them can be found in Ed Krol, *The Whole Internet: User's Guide and Catalog* (Sebastopol, Calif.: O'Reilly and Associates, Inc., 1992). Similarly, an excellent—albeit U.S.-centered—general source on environmental networks is Don Rittner, *Ecolinking: Everyone's Guide to Online Environmental Information* (Berkeley: Peachpit Press, Inc., 1992).

1. An illuminating discussion of the evolution of computers from data-processing machines to personal learning tools is to be found in Howard Rheingold's book *Tools for Thought: The People and Ideas Behind the Next Computer Revolution* (New York: Simon & Schuster, 1985).

2. Svante Arrhenius, "On the Influence of Carbonic Acid in the Air upon the Temperature of the Ground," *Phil. Mag.*, 1896.

3. J.T. Houghton, G.J. Jenkins, and J.J. Ephraums, *Climate Change: The IPCC Scientific Assessment* (Cambridge, United Kingdom: Cambridge University Press, 1990).

4. John Freymann, The Futures Group, Washington, D.C., presentation at the World Wildlife Fund, Washington, D.C., April 20, 1993.

5. Rheingold, op. cit., note 1.

6. The Pentium is rated at 100 MIPs, while the 8086 (the original PC chip) was rated at 0.33 MIPs, according to Terry McManus, Intel Corporation, Chandler, Ariz., private communication, August 12, 1993.

7. Rheingold, op. cit., note 1; 1980 world computers figure is a Worldwatch estimate based on Karen Petska Juliussen and Egil Juliussen, *The 6th Annual Computer Industry Almanac* (Lake Tahoe, Nev.: Computer Industry Almanac, Inc., 1993); world computer and MIPS figures from Egil Juliussen, Computer Industry Almanac, Inc., Lake Tahoe, private communication, July 29, 1993.

8. Juliussen and Juliussen, op. cit., note 7; population figure from Population Reference Bureau, "1993 World Population Data Sheet," Washington, D.C., 1993.

9. As of August 23, 1993, Intel's market value was $26.5 billion, IBM's was $24.6 billion, and and Microsoft's was $22 billion; Microsoft and IBM market values calculated by multiplying number of shares outstanding by share prices; Microsoft sales, share price, and shares outstanding from Ana Krokus, Microsoft Corporation, Redmond, Wash., private communication, August 23, 1993; Intel market value, IBM share price and shares outstanding from "Taking Stock in Intel," *Washington Post*, August 23, 1993; software industry sales from Juliussen

and Juliussen, op. cit., note 7.

10. Computer hardware sales estimate obtained by subtracting estimated software sales in Juliussen and Juliussen, op. cit., note 7, from total computer industry sales estimate (including software) in Stratford Sherman, "The New Computer Revolution," *Fortune,* June 14, 1993.

11. Lenny Siegel, "Analysis of High-Tech Employment Patterns in Eight Leading U.S. High-Tech Centers—1990," fact sheet, Pacific Studies Center, Mountain View, Calif., September, 1992.

12. Unionization from Michael Eisenscher, "Silicon Fist in a Velvet Glove," unpublished paper, December, 1992.

13. Ted Smith, Silicon Valley Toxics Coalition, San Jose, Calif., private communication, August 21, 1993.

14. Edward O. Wilson, *The Diversity of Life* (Cambridge, MA: Harvard University Press, 1992).

15. U.S. Environmental Protection Agency (EPA), Office of Pollution Prevention and Toxics, *1991 Toxics Release Inventory: Public Data Release* (Washington, D.C.: 1993).

16. Ibid.

17. Randolph B. Smith, "Right to Know: A U.S. Report Spurs Community Action by Revealing Polluters," *Wall Street Journal,* January 2, 1991; "Union, Citizens Push for Reductions," *Working Notes on Community Right-to-Know* (Working Group on Community Right to Know, Washington, D.C., July 1990.)

18. Alair MacLean, OMB Watch, Washington, D.C., private communication, August 24, 1993.

19. Deborah A. Sheiman, *The Right To Know More* (Washington, D.C.: National Resources Defense Council, 1991).

20. Canada information from Paul Muldoon, Pollution Probe, Toronto, private communication, August 13, 1993; EC information from Frances Irwin, World Wildlife Fund, Washington, D.C., private communication, August 13, 1993; "Report of the United Nations Conference on Environment and Development: Agenda 21," United Nations Conference on Environment and Development, Rio de Janeiro, June, 1992.

21. Eric Rodenburg, *Eyeless in Gaia: The State of Global Environmental Monitoring* (Washington, D.C.: World Resources Institute, 1992).

22. Such equipment is commonly described and advertised in the environmental engineering trade press; see, for example, the product profiles in *Hazmat World.*

23. Paul Brodeur, "Annals of Chemistry (The Ozone Layer): In the Face of Doubt," *The New Yorker,* June 9, 1986.

24. L. David Mech and Eric M. Gese, "Field Testing the Wildlink Capture Collar on Wolves," *Wildlife Society Bulletin,* vol. 20, pp. 221-223, 1992; K. E. Kunkel et

al., "Testing the Wildlink Activity-Detection System on Wolves and White-Tailed Deer," *Canadian Journal of Zoology*, vol. 69, pp. 2466-2469, 1991.

25. David Leversee, "Cooperative Forest Management: The Sierra Club of Western Canada and British Columbia Ministry of Forests Use Multiple GIS Data Sources to Assess Logging Effects on Vancouver Island," *Earth Observation Magazine*, July/August 1993; Michael Martin et al., "Columbus, Ohio Uses GIS Data for Stormwater Permitting, Utility Development," *Earth Observation Magazine*, March 1993.

26. Congress of the United States, Office of Technology Assessment, *Improving Automobile Fuel Economy: New Standards, New Approaches* (Washington, D.C.: 1991).

27. Alan Thein Durning, "Are You an Eco-Titan?" *World Watch*, March/April 1993; the Global Lab project is thoroughly documented in (and coordinated through) 14 different APC conferences.

28. Greenpeace information from Dick Dillman, Greenpeace, San Francisco, Calif., private communication, August 23, 1993.

29. The archive is called GNET; it resides on a computer at California State University/Dominguez Hills, and is reachable on the Internet at the ftp address [dhvx20.csudh.edu].

30. Number of nodes and users from Michael Stein, San Francisco, Calif., private communication, August 23, 1993; rate of network growth from Howard Rheingold, private communication, March 2, 1993; the U.S. leaders can be reached on the Internet at the electronic mail addresses [president@white-house.gov] and [vice.president@whitehouse.gov], respectively.

31. Internet history from Rheingold, op. cit., note 1; international connections from Larry Landweber, "International Connectivity," fact sheet, April 15, 1993 (available from GNET archive or via ftp at [ftp.cs.wisc.edu]); electronic journals from Michael Strangelove, *Directory of Electronic Journals and Newsletters*, July 1992 (available via ftp from [nisc.sri.com], or in print from Office of Scientific & Academic Publishing, Association of Research Libraries, Washington, D.C.); the special search programs include Gopher, Archie, and WAIS, all of which are described in detail in Ed Krol, *The Whole Internet: User's Guide and Catalog* (Sebastopol, Calif.: O'Reilly and Associates, Inc., 1992).

32. APC networks from Association for Progressive Communications, "Global Computer Communications for Environment, Human Rights, Development, and Peace," brochure (available from GNET archive or in the APC conference [standard]); number of APC users from Michael Stein (see note 30), private communication, August 23, 1993; costs of APC access from International Institute for Sustainable Development (IISD), *Sourcebook on Sustainable Development,* the full text of which may be found in the APC conference [iisd.sourcebk]; the print version may be ordered from IISD, Winnipeg, Manitoba.

33. The bulletins on the Yanomami and on the Malaysian land rights battles were found in the APC's [rainfor.general] conference; the first bulletins on the Yanomami appeared online on August 18th; stories on the same subject appeared in the *New York Times* on August 20th and the *Washington Post* on August 21st.

34. Larry Press, "Relcom, an Appropriate Technology Network," 1992; Bob Travica and Matthew Hogan, "Computer Networking in the USSR: Technology, Uses, and Social Effects," 1992; both articles available from GNET archive.

35. IISD, op. cit., note 32; UNCED documents can be found in the APC conference [en.unced.documents] (in English), [cnumad.documentos] (in Spanish), and [cnued.documents] (in French).

36. Jim Catterson, International Federation of Chemical, Energy and General Workers' Unions (ICEF), Brussels, private communication, June 2, 1993; Jim Catterson, "Electronic Mail for International Solidarity," paper presented at Labourtel UK Conference on Information Technology, Electronic Communications and the Labour Movement, Manchester, United Kingdom, June, 1993.

37. Greenpeace International Waste Trade Project, *The International Trade in Wastes: A Greenpeace Inventory* (Washington, D.C.: 1990); "U.S. Toxic Waste Sold as Fertilizer in Bangladesh," *Toxic Trade Update* (Greenpeace, Washington, D.C.), first quarter, 1993; Heather Spalding, Greenpeace, Washington, D.C., private communication, August 23, 1993.

38. Michael Stein (see note 30), private communication, March 1, 1993; Econet's database collection can be reached from its main menu by typing [d]; International Institute for Energy Conservation, "InfoTree: The Information Transfer Network on Energy Efficiency," undated flyer, Washington, D.C.

39. Alair MacLean (see note 18), private communication, August 23, 1993.

40. U.S. EPA, op. cit., note 15; John Chelen, Unison Institute, Washington, D.C., private communication, July 18, 1993.

41. John Chelen (see note 40), testimony before the Subcommittee on Legislation and National Security and the Subcommittee on Environment, Energy, and Natural Resources, U.S. House of Representatives, May 6, 1993.

42. IISD, op. cit., note 32.

43. The author of this paper serves as an unpaid editorial advisor to the GreenDisk.

44. Sheldon Annis, "Giving Voice to the Poor," *Foreign Policy*, Fall, 1991.

45. Saul Hahn, "The Organization of American States Hemisphere-Wide Networking Intitiative," 1992; Mayuri Odedra et al., "Information Technology in Sub-Saharan Africa," 1993; both articles available from GNET archive.

46. Roy O'Brien, "The APC Computer Networks: Global Networking for Change," *Canadian Journal of Information Science*, July 1992; user numbers from APC user list on Econet.

47. Pascal Renaud and Monique Michaux, "RIO: An Operational Network In 6 Sub-Saharian (sic) Countries of Africa and Three Pacific Islands," paper presented at INET 92, Kobe, Japan, June 15-18, 1992 (available from GNET archive).

48. Randy Bush, "FidoNet: Use, Technology, and Tools," 1992; Mike Jensen and Geoff Sears, "Low Cost Global Electronic Communications Networks for

Africa," paper presented at 34th Annual Meeting of the African Studies Association, St. Louis, Mo., November 1991; both articles available from GNET archive.

49. Gary L. Garriott, "Packet Radio in Earth and Space Environments for Relief and Development," paper presented at 34th Annual Meeting of the African Studies Association, St. Louis, Mo., November 1991; Mark Bennett, University of Zambia, Lusaka, Zambia, private communication, August 18, 1993.

50. Stephen R. Ruth and R. R. Ronkin, "Aiming for the Elusive Payoff of User Networks: An NGO Perspective," paper presented at the annual meeting of the International Society for the Systems Sciences, Denver, Colo., July 12-17, 1992 (available from GNET archive); Garriott, op. cit., note 49.

51. Apple Community Affairs, "Apple in the Community: San Francisco Bay Area and National Programs," undated brochure, Cupertino, Calif.; Albert Langer, "Notes on Computer Communications in Developing Countries," 1991 (available from GNET archive).

52. Michael S. Bergey, "An Overview of Wind Power for Remote Site Telecommunications Facilities," paper presented at Renewable Energy Power Supplies for Telecommunications Conference, British Wind Energy Association, London, United Kingdom, September 25, 1989.

53. Larry Press, "Strategies for Software Export," 1992 (available from GNET archive).

54. Ibid.

55. Odedra et al., op. cit., note 45.

56. Lenny Siegel and John Markoff, *The High Cost of High Tech* (New York: Harper and Row, 1985).

57. Ted Smith (see note 13), private communication, March 3, 1993; Tekla S. Perry, "Cleaning Up," *IEEE Spectrum* (Institute of Electrical and Electronics Engineers), February 1993; Silicon Valley Superfund sites from EPA, Hazardous Site Evaluation Division, "National Priorities List," Washington, D.C., June, 1993; there have been as many as 29 Silicon Valley sites on the Superfund list at any given time; see California Regional Water Quality Control Board, Oakland, Calif., "Alphabetical List of National Priority Cases," October 25, 1991.

58. Siegel and Markoff, op. cit., note 56; Perry, op. cit., note 57; Terry Greene, "Motorola," five-part series of articles from *New Times* (Phoenix, Ariz.), 1992 (available in RTK Net's documents collection).

59. U.S. Department of Labor, Occupational Safety and Health Administration, "29 CFR Part 1910: Occupational Exposure to 2-Methoxyethanol, 2-Ethoxyethanol and Their Acetates (Glycol Ethers); Proposed Rule," *Federal Register*, March 23, 1993; Harris Pastides et al., "Spontaneous Abortion and General Illness Symptoms Among Semiconductor Manufacturers," Journal of Occupational Medicine, July, 1988; Johns Hopkins University, *Retrospective and Prospective Studies of Reproductive Health Among IBM Employees in Semiconductor Manufacturing* (Baltimore: 1993); Shanna H. Swann, California Department of Health Services and University of California, "Reproductive Hazards in

Semiconductor Manufacturing: The Semiconductor Industry Association Series," unpublished manuscript, July, 1993; Fairchild leak study cited in "New IBM Study Shows One-in-Three Semiconductor Workers Suffer Miscarriages," press release of the Campaign for Responsible Technology (CRT), Somerville, Mass., October 12, 1992.

60. Phoenix from Greene, op. cit., note 58; Japan from Kenmochi Kazumi, "High-Tech Pollution," *AMPO Japan-Asia Quarterly Review*, vol. 23, no. 3, 1992; South Korea from *New York Times*, April 16, 1991.

61. Perry, op. cit., note 57.

62. Siegel and Markoff, op. cit., note 56.

63. For Sematech see Perry, op. cit., note 57.

64. Ted Smith (see note 13), private communication, August 21, 1993; United Nations Environment Programme, *Montreal Protocol: 1993 Report of the Technology and Economic Assessment Panel* (New York: 1993).

65. "SEMATECH Gets Campaign Proposals," *The Bargaining Chip* (bulletin of the Electronics Industry Good Neighbor Campaign, a joint project of the Campaign for Responsible Technology (CRT), Somerville, Mass., and the Southwest Network for Environmental and Economic Justice, Albuquerque, New Mexico), April 1993; Rand Wilson, "Bargaining for a New Industrial Policy," undated report, CRT, Somerville, Mass.; Gregory E. Pitts, et al., eds., *Environmental Consciousness: A Strategic Competitiveness Issue for the Electronics and Computer Industry* (Austin, Texas: Microelectronics and Computer Technology Corporation, 1993).

66. EPA, Office of Air and Radiation, "Introducing...EPA Energy Star Computers," fact sheet, November 1992.

67. Steven Anzovin, *The Green PC: Making Choices That Make a Difference* (Toronto: McGraw-Hill, 1993).

68. Ibid.

69. World computer electricity use is a Worldwatch Institute estimate, based on EPA, op. cit., note 66; Department of Energy, *Annual Energy Review 1991* (Washington, D.C.: 1992); Juliussen and Juliussen, op. cit., note 7; Egil Juliussen (see note 7), private communication, July 30, 1993; United Nations, *Energy Statistics Yearbook 1990* (New York: 1992); and Brian Johnson, Energy Star Program, EPA, Washington, D.C., private communication, August 2, 1993.

70. John E. Young, "Asleep on the Job," *World Watch*, March/April, 1993.

71. Brian Johnson (see note 69), private communication, August 2, 1993.

72. Young, op. cit., note 70.

73. Gregory E. Pitts, et al., op. cit., note 65.

74. Anzovin, op. cit., note 67.

75. Federal Minister of the Environment, Nature Conservation, and Nuclear Reactor Safety, Federal Republic of Germany, "Ordinance on the avoidance, reduction and salvage of waste from used electrical and electronic equipment,"

working paper, October 15, 1992.

76. Alex Randall, East-West Education Development Foundation, Boston, Mass., private communication, August 10, 1993; Science, Technology and Development Forum from Dr. Patrick Corr, Department of Computer Science, Queen's University of Belfast (who is the program's coordinator), private communication, August 11, 1993.

77. Hal Sackman, "Computer Workstations: The Occupational Hazard of the 21st Century," paper presented at DIAC-92 (Directions and Implications of Advanced Computing), Berkeley, Calif., May 2-3, 1992.

THE WORLDWATCH PAPER SERIES

_____100. **Beyond the Petroleum Age: Designing a Solar Economy** by Christopher Flavin and Nicholas Lenssen.
_____101. **Discarding the Throwaway Society** by John E. Young.
_____102. **Women's Reproductive Health: The Silent Emergency** by Jodi L. Jacobson.
_____103. **Taking Stock: Animal Farming and the Environment** by Alan B. Durning and Holly B. Brough.
_____104. **Jobs in a Sustainable Economy** by Michael Renner.
_____105. **Shaping Cities: The Environmental and Human Dimensions** by Marcia D. Lowe.
_____106. **Nuclear Waste: The Problem That Won't Go Away** by Nicholas Lenssen.
_____107. **After the Earth Summit: The Future of Environmental Governance** by Hilary F. French.
_____108. **Life Support: Conserving Biological Diversity** by John C. Ryan.
_____109. **Mining the Earth** by John E. Young.
_____110. **Gender Bias: Roadblock to Sustainable Development** by Jodi L. Jacobson.
_____111. **Empowering Development: The New Energy Equation** by Nicholas Lenssen.
_____112. **Guardians of the Land: Indigenous Peoples and the Health of the Earth** by Alan Thein Durning.
_____113. **Costly Tradeoffs: Reconciling Trade and the Environment** by Hilary F. French.
_____114. **Critical Juncture: The Future of Peacekeeping** by Michael Renner.
_____115. **Global Network: Computers in a Sustainable Society** by John E. Young.

_____ **Total Copies**

☐ **Single Copy: $5.00**
☐ **Bulk Copies (any combination of titles)**
    ☐ 2–5: $4.00 ea.   ☐ 6–20: $3.00 ea.   ☐ 21 or more: $2.00 ea.

☐ **Membership in the Worldwatch Library: $25.00 (international airmail $40.00)**
The paperback edition of our 250-page "annual physical of the planet," *State of the World 1993*, plus all Worldwatch Papers released during the calendar year.

☐ **Subscription to *World Watch* Magazine: $15.00 (international airmail $30.00)**
Stay abreast of global environmental trends and issues with our award-winning, eminently readable bimonthly magazine.

No postage required on prepaid orders. Minimum $3 postage and handling charge on unpaid orders.

Make check payable to Worldwatch Institute
1776 Massachusetts Avenue, N.W., Washington, D.C. 20036-1904 USA

Enclosed is my check for U.S. $_____

_____

name   **daytime phone #**

_____

address

_____

city   **state**   **zip/country**